The Gospel According to Norton

The
Gospel According
to
Norton

Grady Nutt

Broadman Press
Nashville, Tennessee

Dewey Decimal Classification: 248.8
Library of Congress Catalog Card Number: 73-91610
Printed in the United States of America

Contents

Frontword

This is my opportunity
to introduce one of my favorite people
to some of my favorite people . . .

Norton was invented
in my rather unconventional mind
as a vehicle
for communicating with seminarians
a very basic truth:
> *far too many*
> *of them*
> *use seminary education*
> *as ammunition*
> *in their young*
> *but ministry-long war*
> *with conservatism*
> > *fundamentalism*
> > *narrow-mindedness*
> or whatever they came out of
> that they are ashamed of
> or in angry disagreement with.

Norton got his name
from the administration building

of The Southern Baptist Theological Seminary
in Louisville, Kentucky.

I attended the school
and graduated
with a Bachelor of Divinity degree
in 1964 . . .
        I stayed on the staff for five years
        to work with prospective students
        and alumni . . .
                I continue to live
                in Louisville
                in close proximity
                to the seminary
                    the staff
                    the administration
                    the students
                    the lovely campus.

I was asked one night
to speak to entering students
in a service at my church . . .
        where I am a member
                    a deacon
                    a layman . . .

The sermon was envisioned by my pastor
as a way to share with students
how our church might be for them
a support force
   rallying point
   encourager
in their student days.

Norton was born for that sermon . . .
        chapter 1 in this book

was my word to them . . .
        the essence
        of the insight
        was:
                the wisest men
                I know
                have a healthy regard
                for what
                they have come out of!

In grappling with Norton
and his relationship with Jesus
I came to some observations
about myself:
        Norton is my *alter ego,*
                my other self . . .
        his relationship with Jesus
        is what I have honestly imagined
        mine or yours might have been
        if we had been there
        to walk and talk with him.

In thinking about that
I began to free up a great deal
in thinking about the biblical stories
I had grown up on . . .
        I started asking new questions
                looking further
                probing
        quite as I had been encouraged to do
        in my seminary training.

My own preaching
        talking
        conference-leading
        banquet-speaking

started to take on the character
of Norton . . .
     I started to feel at home
     with Nicodemus
         Zacchaeus
         Thomas
         Simon . . .

Out of that freer climate
this book was born
in my parents' bathtub
on a lazy afternoon . . .
               just soaking . . .

It occurred to me
that I could tell these stories
in the character of Norton
and let you (astute reader that you are!)
see beyond miracles
         majesty
         Messiah
a few freckles
     frowns
     funnings
in the Holy Bible.

Here I owe a debt of gratitude
to some of the most influential
and helpful friends I have ever had . . .
     the staff of the department
     of National Student Ministries
     of the Sunday School Board
     of the Southern Baptist Convention
     in Nashville, Tennessee . . .
more specifically
     to Norman Bowman

and Denise Jones . . .
editors of *The Student* . . .

The Student
is a publication
directed specifically
at college students
with stimulating articles
regular columns
excellent artwork
superb features.

I say without reservation
that *The Student*
is the most aware
alert
provocative
free-swinging
exciting
publication produced by Southern Baptists!

Denise and Norman called me one day
to suggest a regular column of humor
for a new format of the magazine:
the result was a series
with the title of this book—
THE GOSPEL ACCORDING TO NORTON.

Their faith and patience
allowed me to write a story each month . . .
their generosity
also allowed me "first copy" privileges:
this meant I could take the columns
and compile them
for this book.

That has taken longer
than the original stories!

Therefore, *Norton!*

It is a genuine pleasure to have
      Sharon Baugh
      of Dallas, Texas,
      do the artwork for *Norton* . . .
            she heard me discuss him once
            and sketched him for me . . .
                  he's looked that way
                  ever since!

Sharon and I collaborated on my first book,
      Being Me,
and I owe a great deal of credit
for its acceptance to her work . . .
            therefore, *we* are pleased
            to bring you Norton.

Nancy Ammerman typed the manuscript . . .
            she does not deserve *thanks:*
            she deserves a crown!
                  I *think* a bit weird . . .
                  I *write* strange!

After you've read Norton
I'll be back with a word
called the "Backword"
on page 93.

Now, be kind to Norton . . .
            he's rather special
            to me . . .

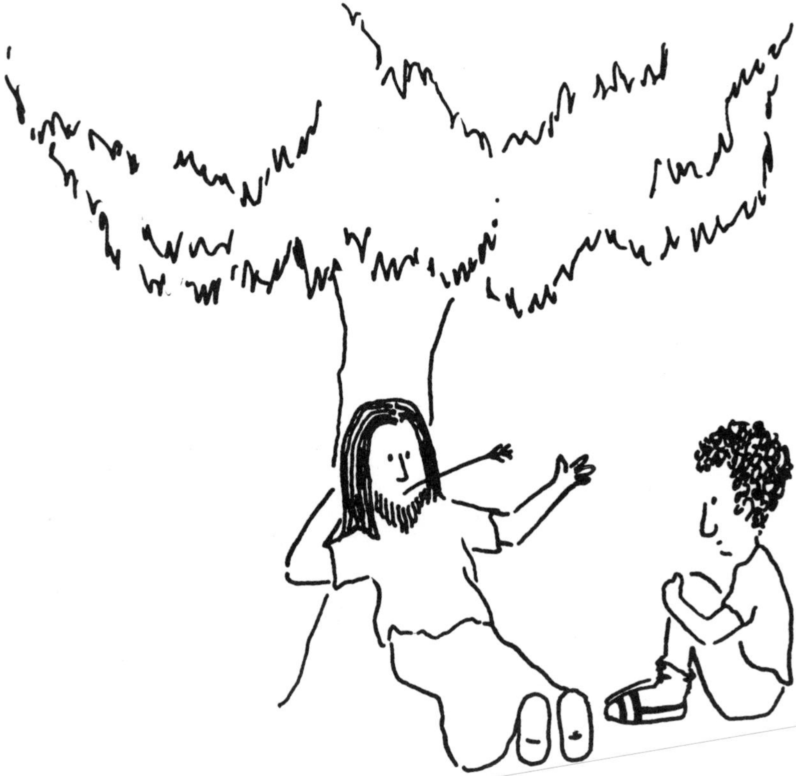

1 Norton

I would like to tell you the story
    of my relationship
    to Jesus of Nazareth . . .
        carpenter
        teacher
        friend
    and some stories
    of several special people
    who touched his life
    and were touched
    by his life . . .
        and some stories
        he loved to tell
        in his own
        incredible way.

Let me introduce myself, first . . .
    the name is *Norton*
        no middle initial
        no last name
    just *Norton.*

I grew up on the south side of Jerusalem
        in a state
        of discontent.

Many folks—especially my parents—
        considered me
        unusual
                eccentric
                    way out
                        strange . . .
                            I kept my hair cut short
                            wore mini-togas
                            grew no beard
                            wore socks with my sandals!

(The whole thing kept my Dad
in a constant uproar . . .
        "You just don't do that!"
        "What will people think?"
        "You look weird!")

You might say
        I had a passion
            for fashion!
I was, otherwise, typical
        of south Jerusalem youth . . .
            snitched a little fruit
            played in the streets
            liked girls
            hung around the market . . .

One fairly-ordinary-Thursday-night
        in Jerusalem
        changed
        my life . . .

My best friend, Ephraim, suggested

that we go
out to the river
to hear
a really way-out
aesthetic
    hermit
       preacher
          named
          John
          the
          Baptist . . .
               his message
               was mainly
               anti-Pharisee . . .
       I was pro-anybody who was
               anti-Pharisee!

Ephraim—or, "Eef," as we called him—
    had heard him speak already
    and really liked him . . .
        I was skeptical
        but curious . . .
             so we went
             together.

I felt a bit awkward going out like this
    but I didn't
    have a great deal to do—
        funny how many good things
        have come my way
        just as unexpectedly . . .

John was all and more than I'd expected . . .
    and he made me
    feel ordinary
    in his free-spirit clothes:
        double-breasted camel hair suit

(wrong-side out)
platform high-top sandals
teased hair
the works . . .
                    a health food fan
                    diet of bugs and honey
                        preached like
                        he'd had
                        half-a-cup
                        of crickets!

The first night by the river
        was the beginning
        of a deep friendship
        with John . . .
                    in only four days
                    I was arriving
                    early enough
                    to get
                    a front rock!

In short, I became an ardent follower . . .
        he was my hero—
                        great dresser
                        unique
                        distinctive
                        outspoken
                        honest.

I tried more and more to be like him . . .
        and he really liked me
                liked the way I dressed
                            thought
                            questioned . . .
                liked my flair
                    for the unusual . . .
        we really got close.

I was with John the afternoon he baptized Jesus . . .
    I was amazed at John's attitude
        at his strange statements
        ". . . should let you baptize me . . ."
        ". . . not worthy to tie your shoes . . ."
        at his general sense of awe.

The baptism completed, they stood quietly in the river
    drip-drying
    gazing quietly into the sky
        as though
        they heard
        sounds I
            couldn't
            hear . . .
                I strained
                and heard
                zero . . .

Jesus left silently
        pensively
    and I walked over to John
    to probe the moment . . .

John was moody.
He didn't want to talk.
He cut me short
    and walked off
    up the river bank
    and sat on a large rock
    all afternoon . . .
        the mood lasted
        for days
        and weeks . . .
            I was
            bewildered.

Word eventually reached me
      that Jesus had a group
      following him
          and meeting
          with frequency
          further back up the river . . .
              one night
              I went
              to "scout" the new teacher
                  and his followers.

The first night I heard him
      it happened!
              . . . here was the Messiah
                about whom John
                had been preaching!
      in just three visits
      I transferred
      my membership!

I spent more and more time with Jesus
      and did chores
          and errands
              for him and his disciples . . .
                  these were
                  among the most meaningful
                  days of my life . . .
                        new thoughts
                        fresh ideas
                        comrades
                        laughter
                        spiritual deepening
                        warmth . . .
          he took me into his confidence
          and had many
              many long talks

about his understanding
of life
God
himself.

One such talk was *the* talk
that really
changed
my
life . . .

It had been a hard day
multitudes
questions
and multitudes of questions . . .

He was sitting by a large tree
dangling his feet
in the cool river water
and chewing
a long
fuzzy weed . . .
one of his
favorite habits . . .
the moonlight
twinkled in his eyes
like sparks
from
a
campfire . . .

I sat by him and stirred the river with a limb
and we talked
of many things . . .
then he asked me
if I had seen John
lately . . .

I chuckled.
He frowned . . .
        then he asked me why I chuckled
        to which I replied:
                "Oh, he's still wearing that double-breasted
                camel hair suit
                and preaching blisters on his throat . . ."
                        and other
                                curt
                                sarcastic things—

Without looking I felt his eyes on me . . .
        I turned
        to meet them
        straight on . . .

"Norton, do you know where you'd be
        if it
        hadn't been
        for John?"
                and I blushed
                        squirmed
                        and
                        dropped my eyes . . .
        "Still snitching fruit
                hanging around the market . . ."
        "Exactly," he said . . .
                                and at that point
                                taught me
                                one of the greater lessons
                                I've ever learned:
                                        The young idealist
                                        is frequently guilty
                                        of finding his Messiah
                                        and then spending his time
                                        belittling his Forerunner!

He showed me that the wise man
    gives proper appreciation
    in his life to his past . . .
        learns to sift the sawdust of heritage
        in order to find the nuggets
            that make the current moment
            have any meaning.
In short, if I had not met John
    I probably would not
    have met Jesus!
    I never knocked John again . . .
        in fact,
        I loved him
        more than ever!

As I traveled with Jesus through his brief ministry
    I gained the special thrill
    of being part of his inner circle . . .
        and *daily* thanked God
        for John . . .
            and now, I'd like
            to tell you some of my
            favorite memories . . .
                the style is informal
                the content is basically
                    informed imagination . . .
                come along with me . . .
                        socks
                      optional!

2 Nicodemus

Jesus and I were sitting together
     in an olive grove
     outside Jerusalem.
          It was near midnight
          and we were eating
          some fish
               and dry bread
          Mary and Martha
          had fixed for us
               that afternoon
               in Bethany . . .

The coals of the fire glowed softly
          and brightened slightly
          as the gentle
               Palestinian
               breeze
                    stroked
                    them . . .

The conversation was light—
      we'd really had a busy day
      and a long afternoon walk—
         it was good
         to relax . . .

Simon and some of the others
      were down the hill
      a bit
      in a small lean-to
      they'd constructed . . .

Simon called up the hill:
      "Someone to see you,
      Jesus . . ."
         Jesus cocked his head
         to one side
         and looked puzzled—
            a "who-could-that-be-
            at-this-time-of-night"
            kind of look . . .

Twigs snapped underfoot—
A long bejewelled robe
      returned the campfire's
      warm hello
         with
         neutral
         sparkles . . .

He came closer—
      and I recognized
      Nicodemus—
         ruling elder
         of the Jews
            Pharisee
            Most Important!

I made as if to leave
    but Jesus smiled
    put his hand on my knee
        and gave me a
        "Stay-where-you-are-it's-ok-Norton"
        kind of gesture . . .

I must admit it—
I was excited!
    I had been with him
    for several weeks now
        and this was the first time
        I'd seen him encounter
        a really big leader!

Nicodemus was uneasy;
Jesus lifted his eyebrows
    opened one hand
    in a gesture
    intended to give
                Nicodemus
                openers . . .

"Now, Jesus, we know you are a remarkable man
    with rare gifts
    for teaching
    and
    for doing great
        and mighty
        works . . .
            even though
            you didn't go to seminary!"

Jesus looked at me ever so swiftly
    and
    smiled at me
    with his eyes . . .

Then he spoke to Nicodemus:
    "Nicodemus—
        You must be
        born again."

Nicodemus seemed miffed:
    "Look my good fellow—
        I came
        all the way
        out here
        for a serious conversation
            and you start
                playing riddles
                with me . . .
        return to my mother's womb—
                    indeed!
        Would you
        please try
        to make some sense!"

"I never made more sense, Nicodemus,"
    he replied—
        "Sit here
        beside me
        and let's
            talk
            about it . . ."

Nicodemus lifted his robes
    and sat
        on a large rock
        by the fire . . .
                the
                session
                began—

it was one
of the most beautiful moments
I can remember
in all my time
with him . . .

He was always trying to cool down
my hostility
which boiled freely
whenever
I got around
any of the
Establishment leaders.

I couldn't avoid the clear lesson
in his
"Stay-where-you-are-it's-ok-Norton"
gesture:
He was teaching *me*
while
he was talking with Nicodemus.

The lesson was plain:
His gospel had to be experienced—
not argued!

I would have loved nothing more
than to lock concepts
with Nicodemus—
really show him
the hypocrisy
of the whole system
of ritual
rule

piety
observance—

Jesus—on the other hand—talked with him
        about
        that part of his life
        that blocked his relationship
                        to God—
                Nicodemus
                was a Jew of the Jews
                        and thought himself
                        in right relationship
                                to God
                                        because
                                        of his
                                        earth-birth . . .

Jesus said that a man must be
        of his own will
        born a second time
                from above
                        or he cannot be
                        rightly related
                                to God—

Much later that evening they concluded
        their conversation—
                Nicodemus
                was in a
                somber mood . . .
                                I saw him
                                several times
                                in the next
                                few weeks . . .

On that horrible Friday—
        the worst day
        of my life—

when Jesus
was executed
I was startled
to get a message
from Nicodemus . . .
He wanted me
to come to his home
right away . . .

He wanted to know what plans had been made
for the burial
of Jesus—
I told him
Joseph from Arimathea
had offered
a new tomb—
He asked me
to take him
to Joseph . . .

I led him quickly to Joseph—
They gripped forearms
and looked quietly
into each other's eyes . . .

The town was shocked
when the body of Jesus
was taken
from the cross
and was carried away
by Joseph
and *Nicodemus!*
and Nicodemus
had brought a king's ransom
in spices and ointments!

I carried these for him

as he carried
the feet of Jesus
all the way through
the streets
    of
    Jerusalem!

Not a word was spoken—
    An occasional sob/sniff
    parted the drape
        of silence—
            I never
            have known
            that kind of pain and hurt
                before or since . . .

The road to Joseph's tomb
    took us right past
    the olive grove
        where Nicodemus
         first met Jesus—
            He paused
            The procession stopped
            Nicodemus looked
                quietly
                up the hill . . .

Then he turned and looked at me
    and through his tears—
        He
        smiled
        at
        me
        with
        his
        eyes . . .

3 The Woman at the Well

Really—it had been a funny morning!
We left Jerusalem early
        heading for Galilee
            a trip
            that was to shatter
                    tradition
                        ritual
                            habit
                                prejudice
                and
                Simon!

The normal Jerusalem-Galilee route
        for the self-respecting Jew
        was due east from Jerusalem
            across the Jordan river
            north up the east bank
            back across the river
                just south of
                the Sea of Galilee
        thereby
                avoiding the land
                of *Samaria* . . .

Jesus caught us all off guard
     surprised us completely
     turned due north
          right outside
          the Jerusalem
          east gate
     and headed
          right for Samaria!

Simon almost developed
     a permanent twitch!
       He argued loud
          long
       and climaxed
          his furious debate
          with an unbelievable
              burst of logic:
          "But there are
          Samaritans
          up there!"
       to which Jesus responded:
          (twinkle in eye)
          "So . . .?"

Simon looked from frantic face
          to frantic face
     and finally came up with:
              "Well . . . they just
              hide behind rocks
              waiting to leap out
              and be Samaritans
              right in front of you!"
Jesus finally dropped his head
    as tears of laughter
    welled up in his eyes

as his shoulders
began to shake
        at last
        bursting forth
        in gales of laughter!
The whole group joined in—
        finally Simon was
        laughing harder
        than anyone!

Such was his way to back you up
        into the corner
        of absurdity!
                (It really
                bewildered the Pharisees!)

We crossed the border into Samaria;
        Jesus stopped
        before we reached
        a huge boulder:
                "Simon—
                would you
                like to check behind . . ."
                        . . .

"All right! All right!" he chuckled . . .
        The group laughed
                elbowed Simon good-naturedly
        Jesus winked at me
                and we walked on . . .

At noon we came to a well outside Sychar—
        a Samaritan village.
                The well
                was called
                "Jacob's well!"

Jesus sat down . . . rubbed the back of his neck . . .
  and said:
    "I'm hungry . . ."
  Simon nearly passed out!
    "If we'd gone around
    we could have found food."
  Jesus was sure
  there'd be food here.
    "In *Samaria?*"
    shouted Simon . . .
  Jesus answered (twinkle in eye)
        (calmly)
    "In Samaria. . . ."

Simon and the rest of the group left—
  I stayed
  with Jesus . . .

They had been gone about fifteen minutes
  when a woman from town
  approached the well
    carrying a huge waterpot
    on her shoulder . . .
      It was empty
      but
      it carried like full . . .

Her features were hard
  her gait was lifeless
  her eyes were dark
        sockets
        of
        weariness . . .

Most women came to the well in groups—
      early in the morning
      in the cool of the day—

This woman
came alone
at *noon*
    in the heat of the day . . .
                you didn't need ESP
                to know she
                        had
                        trouble!
                to know she
                        was
                        a
                        forced
                        loner!

She lowered her waterpot
        and started to pull it up—
                its excess
                sloshed back
                into the well's innards . . .
        Jesus stopped her in mid-draw
        with:
                "Could I trouble you for a drink?"

Her sarcasm was like cold
                        thick
                        honey . . .
        He finally convinced her
        he was for real
        and not just trying to con her—
                She extended a cup . . .

He drank long and deep
        then looked at her
        while watching the cup
                (He was a master at that!)
            "I know a well

you could drink from
and you'd never
be thirsty again. . . ."
She snapped back:
"Look friend,
they don't invent
running water 'til 1868!"

Then he unfolded a beautiful lesson to her:
The well of God's forgiveness
never runs dry
always springs
to newness within . . .
And it finally dawned on her:
This is the Messiah!

She rushed to town and they all followed her back:
If you can't hide trouble
you surely can't hide joy!

People who wouldn't walk with her
in the cool of the day
ran out with her
in the heat of noon!

They surrounded Jesus at the well
and heard him use it as a parable:
The well of God's forgiveness
has three compartments—
(1) God forgives and accepts us
(2) The community must
forgive and accept us
(3) We must forgive and accept ourselves!

About that time Simon and friends returned
with a fish
at arm's length

Jesus teased him again a little
and pointed out
        that if that Samaritan fish
        had made it thirty miles
        further down the Jordan River
        he'd have been Jewish!

Then—Jesus dropped his final blockbuster—
        We stayed two more *days*
                two more *nights*
                        in Sychar!

Simon
almost
cried!

When Jesus announced his intention
        to stay longer
        in Sychar,
                the Mayor
                stepped forward
                and offered us
                a place to stay
                in his home—
                        Jesus thanked him
                        for his courtesy
                        and told him
                        he had other plans—
                                You've already guessed
                                where we stayed—
                                        in the home
                                        of the woman
                                        he'd met at the well!

(Not many of us mind being seen
        at the wells of life
        with the outcasts

of society—
few of us
would stay
in the home
of a woman like this
        to
        teach
        a
        town
        how
        to love!)

Jesus walked through the crowd
        with the woman
                once hated
                        ridiculed
                                belittled
        and started back toward Sychar—
                over and over again
                women smiled
                        waved tiny waves.

I was walking behind them
        close enough
        to hear her sniff occasionally
        to see her dab
                at her eyes.

We neared town and I looked back
        at the townsfolk
                following us
                along the trail—
        and had to smile
                and nudge Jesus . . .

There was Simon
            among the *Samaritans*
        carrying
        the waterpot!

He looked up
        saw Jesus smile
        blushed
            and
            winked . . .

4 The Cleansing of the Temple

I never ceased to be amazed at the intensity
        of Jesus' emotions—
                he was simultaneously
                the most gentle
                        and awesome
                                person I've ever known . . .
                he could hold a blossom
                                to his nostrils
                                as a mother
                                might kiss the forehead
                                of her child
                                at bathtime—
                he could also scowl the fear of God
                                into a statue!

I was always curious about his anger—
        usually so controlled
                        disciplined—
                no time
                stands out
                like my first trip
                with him
                to the Temple . . .

We had been to Capernaum for a visit
    with his family
    for a wedding in Cana
            where he astonished everyone
            by turning water into wine—
                    (strangely, he never
                            seemed to want
                            to talk about it
                            with anyone . . .)

We arrived in Jerusalem for the Passover Feast
    and he headed
    straight for the Temple—
        today there was
        an unusual quiet
        about him
            as we walked
            through the bustling streets
            teeming with crowds
            readying for the great festival . . .
        the crowds were boisterous
                    thick
                    jostling—
        he was like
        the center of a storm—
                steady
                eyes straight ahead
                introspective . . .

His brow furrowed
        eyes moved a fraction deeper in their sockets—
            we were nearing
            the entrance of the Temple—

It was a moment of pain and shock to him
        (I am certain of that . . .)

when he entered
and found ourselves
in the court of the Gentiles—
  here were tables set up
      for changing
      out-of-Jerusalem money
      to Temple currency
          (for an immodest fee!)
  here were animals being sold
      for special sacrifices
      to replace animals
      brought by worshipers—
          (animals which never
          seemed capable
          of passing
          Temple inspection!)
  here were arguments
      smells
      noises
      marketplace atmosphere—
all in a place
      meant
      for worship!

I saw him stop—
I felt him stiffen—
I sensed his smouldering anger!

You can understand this better—perhaps—
    if I set the scene for you more clearly—

Jews came from all over the known world
    to attend the Passover Feast days—
        they brought money
        from their various provinces—
            each was assessed a tax

for the operation
of the Temple—
only Temple currency was acceptable
for such a tax
therefore it was a practice
to convert foreign money
to Temple money—
a handsome profit was taken
for this necessary service . . .

The ritual of worship centered around
the sacrifice of animals
only approved animals were acceptable—
approved animals were for sale
few animals from outside
were able to pass
the critical
examination—
arguments were
the order of the day—
loud voices
oaths
animal sounds and smells
all blending into
something less
than the ideal atmosphere
for silence and worship . . .

Jesus saw and heard this—
but his attention was caught—
as usual—
by the
usually unnoticed:
a young couple
kneeling near the wall

that separated the Gentiles
from the other courts
provided for the Jews
to use
for worship . . .
They were huddled together
trying to make contact
with the God of the Jews—

Jesus looked with tenderness
and affection on their bent
humble
forms . . .

About this same moment, a hotheaded man
from upper Galilee
and an official animal inspector
got into a loud
vulgar argument
over the alleged
imperfection
of a pair of pigeons
brought
for
sacrifice . . .

Pushing
and
shoving ensued
and the visitor from Galilee
was knocked to the ground
right across
the ankles
of the young Gentile woman
praying at the wall . . .
a donkey next to them

whirled and knocked over
a water jar
where they were kneeling . . .
in the swirling dust and noise
Jesus
suddenly came to life!
furiously!

He dashed over to the fighting men—
now screaming
and yelling
and hitting—
and pulled them apart
by their collars
and held them back
as a fisherman might hold up
two fish caught on the same line!

The men were startled at his strength
at his authority
at his anger
at his look of pain . . .

He pushed them back from the kneeling couple—
the anger in his eyes
flashed
like
sparks
from
an
anvil!

With a sudden
unexpected move
he kicked over
a rickety table

                    covered with coins
                    and rolls of parchment . . .
          he looked up
          to see one of the animal-tenders
          swing a whip at him—
                    he sidestepped
                    the whiplash
                              caught the man's wrist
                              in one hand
                              squeezed so hard
                              the man dropped to his knees
                                    whimpering in pain—

Then Jesus took the whip from the man's hand
          turned around
          snapped it with a loud *crack*
                    over the crowd's heads
                    and then
                    started unpenning "perfect" animals!

He drove sheep
                    pigeons
                    bull calves before him
                              right down
                              the Temple steps—
                    owners dashed frantically about
                    trying to recorral
                    their lost flocks
                              money changers
                              shoved coins into leather pouches
                              ducked past him
                              darted down the streets
                                    in fear
                                          anger

righteous indignation . . .
he smouldered
like a cooling volcano
and shouted
like I never
heard him shout
before
or since:
"You have turned
my father's
house of prayer
into a
den of thieves!"

The crowd disappeared
like dry leaves
before a
driving wind . . .

Silence prevailed . . .
heads hung in shame . . .

He herded sheep
goats
oxen
pigeons all out the royal porch gate . . .
then he turned
to the young couple . . .

They were staring in shock . . .
I gaped in amazement . . .
He breathed hard for a few moments . . .
then he smiled his patented
patient smile—
they and I
returned it . . .

He chatted with them several moments
        won their admiration
                confidence . . .
                        then he said:
                                "Why don't we
                                all pray together . . ."
                We did . . .

And I felt strangely
        like
        a
        blossom
        in
        gentle hands . . .

5 Zacchaeus

The night was cool . . .
The breeze was gentle . . .
The day had been eventful . . .
The disciples were loose . . .
Our spirits were high . . .

Simon and I were sitting together
        talking about
        Jesus' conversation
        earlier that day
            with a
                wealthy
                young
                ruler.

Jesus interrupted everyone to announce
        his plans for the coming day:
            "I have decided
            to go down
            to
            Jerusalem
            tomorrow."

This would mean a long
                    hot walk . . .
        so we turned in early
            and soon were fast asleep. . . .
                    Early next morning
                    we were
                    up and on our way.

At noon we were approaching Jericho . . .
        I was walking
        between Jesus and Matthew
                    when Matthew said:
            "Oh, Master—
                    there is a man
                    here in Jericho
                    I want you to meet
                    if we have time. . . ."
        Jesus said (with a smile):
            "Certainly we have time,
            Matthew—
                    Who is he?"

Matthew told this brief story:
        The man's name was Zacchaeus—
            small in stature
            big of heart . . .
        he was the tax collector
            for Jericho . . .
        Matthew had met him in March
            at a tax collector's
                    convention
            in Joppa.

Matthew had spent a great deal of time
        with Zacchaeus
        at the convention

and developed
great appreciation
for him—
    the reason was that
    Zacchaeus had applied
    for the tax post
    after the last collector
    died suddenly.
        Zacchaeus thought
        someone should have
        the job who would not
        take advantage
        of the position
        but would perform
        the duty within
        the limits of the law.

So he took the job to bring integrity
    to tax collecting . . .
        but the "Jerichohabitants"
        never saw beyond his title
        and belittled him
            ridiculed him
            refused to associate with him
                    (publicly or
                        privately)
            burned Stars of David
            in
            his grass!

He was a lonely man
        but he kept his job
        so unscrupulous persons
        would not again
        take advantage
        of Jericho!

Jesus was greatly impressed!
    "We must look him up—
   sounds like
        our kind
        of people!"

Word spread quickly in Jericho
    that Jesus was in the town—
        crowds lined the streets
        in an effort to see him.

It was always hard for me
    to be humble and quiet
    when we were
    the center of attention . . .

Along the way I saw a man's head
    sticking up over the crowd—
        it was obviously
        a small man
            and he was standing
            in the fork
            of a
            medium-sized tree
            straining to see Jesus . . .

I recognized him immediately
    from Matthew's description—
        I nudged Jesus
        with my elbow—
            He looked past my nod
            and smiled.

He walked through the pressing crowd
    stopped before the surprised man
    and said:
        "Zacchaeus?"

His left eyebrow
         and voice
                rose slightly
as he said the name.

Zacchaeus nearly fell from his perch
        in surprise—
                "How did you know . . .?"
He started the question
        then Matthew appeared
        beside Jesus.
                Zacchaeus laughed
                        jumped down
                        embraced Matthew
                and invited us
                all
                        to his house
                        for dinner.

The crowd was floored
        and angry!

The visit in Zacchaeus' home
        was a beautiful encounter—
                Jesus began the conversation
                by telling Zacchaeus
                what a fine thing
                he thought his work was
                        what a good thing
                        for Jericho.

It turned out that he'd been giving
        half his income
        to charitable causes
                and he had a rare policy
                that if he erred
                in computing

a man's tax
he multiplied
the return
by four!

When Jesus learned this—he beamed!
"It makes
the heart of God
glad
when men
live like this,
Zacchaeus—
I, too, know the loneliness
that comes when your actions
cause your fellowman
to shun you
and misunderstand you!"

It was precisely this attitude of Jesus
that caused Zacchaeus
to open his life
to the gospel—
the good news
that God loves each of us
with all his heart. . . .

Zacchaeus said:
"You are the first person
who claims to serve God
who has understood
what I'm up to. . . .
There have been times
when *the righteous* of Jericho
have made me wonder
if it was worth
the trouble!"

We prepared to leave about mid-afternoon—
       It was obvious
       that both Jesus
              and Zacchaeus
                     hated to part . . .
              They embraced
              in the front yard
                     and promised
                     somehow
                     sometime
                            they'd
                            get together
                            again . . .

"What did you think, Master?"
       It was Matthew—
              anxious
              excited
                     to feel out
              Jesus' reactions
              to Zacchaeus . . .

Jesus smiled at Matthew and said:
       "No man
       who lives like that
       is ever small
       in God's eyes!
              Thank you
                     Matthew—
              for calling him
              to my attention!"

I was pleased to have been there that day—
       Zacchaeus remains
       one of my close friends—
              I stay there often

when I travel
through Jericho. . . .
    We love to swap stories
    about our contacts
    with Jesus. . . .
Zacchaeus
became the lay-leader
of the church in Jericho—
        because of him
        all men were welcome!

Jesus' encounter with Zacchaeus
        taught me a lesson
        that is prime with me
        'til this day—
            The critics of sinners
            are never
            the redeemers of sinners!

Even small men looked big
        when you looked at them
        his way!

6 Of Soil and Seed

It was a sunny spring day . . .
  we were with Jesus
  on the southwest bank
  of the Sea of Galilee.

I had been with Jesus
  and his disciples
  only a few weeks . . .
    I was absolutely overwhelmed
    by the crowds
    he had begun to attract—
      this was the
      largest crowd
      I had seen yet.

I asked Peter how many people
  he thought
  might be here today—
    he said
    Jesus never counted multitudes!

Then he grinned and scratched his beard . . .
  "Can't you see it,

Norton . . .
start wasting all that time
                         energy
                         effort
        keeping records
        on multitudes!
                First thing you know
                we'd never get
                any good accomplished
                trying to make studies
                        and reports
                on why the multitude
                        was off
                        ten percent
                        last night!"

Then he grinned . . .
        I grinned back . . .
He slapped my back . . .
        we set about
            settling the group down.

The crowd was really lively that day—
        the basic question
        was clearly:
            "Who are you, really—
        What are you up to?"

He told my favorite parable that day
                        to answer that question. . . .
I never ceased to marvel at the way
        he could pull
        a perfect story
        out of the air
            to answer

such deep questions . . .
this was the
very reason
why he was called
"Teacher . . ."

This time he spotted a farmer
at work in a field
in the distance—
"Who are you . . .
What are you up to . . .?"
He pointed to the farmer
and said to the multitude:
"See that farmer there?"

They turned to look—
(you can *hear* a multitude
turn to look!)
turned back
and nodded as a group . . .

"My work is something like that . . .
sowing the seeds
of God's love . . ."
and
the parable
moved on . . .

It lives on in my memory
almost word
for word
like I heard him
tell it that way . . .

When the day had drawn to a close
    and we were alone,
    I had a chance
    to probe him further
    about the parable . . .
        he never
        gave his interpretations
        away easily.

"You talked about hard soil
                good soil on solid rock
                    soil full of weeds
                        and thorns
           and good soil . . ."
    from there
    I started pressing him
    for deeper insight—
        on each of the soils
        he opened me
        to new insights
        about him
        about myself—

I saw many things that day
    that have continued
    to change my life.

On the surface Jesus was saying
    he was like the farmer
    the seed was the gospel
    the soils represented hearers—
                hearers
                    of different kinds.

I began to share with him
      how I saw each of the soils
      and how I understood God
      with respect to each of them . . .

For instance:
      (1) The hard soil
            was not just
            the determined
            opponent of God
                this soil got hard
                from heavy traffic—
                    it was
                    a hard path
                    a beaten way
      I surmised that it might be possible
          for a person
          to become so busy
          doing even *good* things
              that he might cease
              being open to God's gifts . . .
          for a person to starve
              serving multitudes
              from a full kettle . . .

He smiled and added:
      "Some people are so busy
      observing ritual
      that they never get to know God personally—
          ritual must bring me
          to close
              personal contact with God
          or it's useless

(2) The shallow layer of good soil
          on a layer
          of solid rock
          intrigued me . . .
               I concluded
               that each of us
               faces crisis situations
               that test our "roots" in God—
     He agreed . . .

He went on to say
     that only deep dirt
     could hold roots . . .
          most of us go through the motions
          of spiritual maturing
          and do not deepen
          in our expressions of his love
                         to his world . . .
          his next statement has stayed with me:
               "If I say I love God
               and don't evidence it in my life,
               I'm a liar!"
He couldn't separate deed and creed!

(3) He said I caught the point of the third soil
          right on the head!
               it was full of weeds
               and thorns . . .
          I guessed he meant
          that often our lives are strangled
          by things that don't matter ultimately—
               he often referred
               to people who dwelt

in this strange state of mind
as "nit-pickers!"

He felt that more people lost the joy
of their faith in God
because of pet attitudes
over nonsense!
that always strangles life and love.

(4) The good soil—
productive
fertile
abundant
rich
loamy—
I began to interpret
how I saw this part of the parable
trying to appear humble
even though
I was
in
the
inner circle. . . .

He pressed me hard
he kept tantalizing me
to try to find
the deepest lesson
of the parable . . .
it finally hit me:
All the soils
were in
same field!

He slapped my knee
    threw his head back in a hearty laugh—
      "You have it!"

And surely I did . . .
    my life is a blend of *many* responses to God
      busy in solid service
        but like a hustling cook
        sometimes hungry
        over a full kettle . . .
      living in a shallow
          artificial faith at times . . .
      overly concerned at times
        with things
        that don't matter ultimately . . .
      and—like now—warm and fertile soil
        productive
        responsive to his bidding . . .

He smiled—
    and my roots dug deeper—
      my branches stretched for the clouds . . .

For a carpenter—
    he
    was
    some
    kind
    of
    farmer . . .

7 The Good Samaritan

It was a sixty-four shekel question—
      well thought out
      obviously calculated
      keenly prepared . . .

The questioner was a man I'd noticed
      on the fringe
      of our following
          ever since
          we'd entered Jerusalem on this trip . . .

It came about like this:

We had just come from a great time in Galilee—
      Jesus' miracles
          and insights
      had staggered even those of us
      in his closest followers . . .
          I know
          I was with him to the bitter end . . .
              however
              whenever that might be . . .

Out of the fame and massive crowds
    we headed south
    from Galilee
    to Jerusalem
        through Samaria—
            we lunched in Sychar
            with our new friend
            we'd met earlier
            at the well . . .
                she was delighted
                to see us all!

Other Samaritan villages were not so hospitable—
    a few of the disciples
    got angry on two or three occasions
    at our receptions—
        he calmed them
            reminding them over and over
            that we had much to accomplish . . .

His urgency was a mystery to me . . .

Mystery intensified . . .
    "Who do folks say I am?"
        Simon:
            "The Messiah!
            The Son of the Living God!"

    A strange disappearance
        up a mountain for a day
            with Peter, James, and John—
        their wide-eyed silence
        upon return—

Many references to last days
        to *time-at-hand* . . .
   I followed in slack-jawed amazement!

Now, into Jerusalem . . .
   his advance of "two-by-twos"
   had alerted every village
             hamlet
             town
   that he was coming their way—
here we faced our largest throng . . .
   for several days
   the questions came fast
          furious . . .

The man I mentioned earlier
   appeared on the edges of the crowd
   in Jerusalem
   with probing—doubt—challenge
      written all over his face . . .

On three different occasions
   when Jesus was talking
   about every man's importance to God
      this man swallowed hard
      as if to leap into the discussion—
         he bit his lip each time
         and kept his silence . . .

I mentioned him to Jesus a couple of times . . .
   he'd only smile
   and pat me on the shoulder . . .

One day it finally happened:
        Jesus had told the crowd
        the day before
        that he'd be at the foyer of the five porches
        the next day about mid-morning . . .

When we walked up, the man was ready
        and raised the first question:
                "May I ask you
                a question,
                sir?"
        Jesus said:
                "Certainly—
                what is it?"

The man began:
        "I'm a lawyer—
        I'm interested in your opinion—
        How shall I find eternal life, teacher?"
                no biting sarcasm
                no harsh ridicule
                no cynicism—
                        a fair question . . .

It was—however—the kind of question
        men often ask
        in order to *say*
        rather than to *hear* something . . .

Jesus picked it up immediately:
        "How do *you* read the law,
        my friend?"

The man was a bit flustered . . .
    "We all know that—
        'Love God with all your heart
        and your neighbor as yourself . . .'
        Do you agree?"

"I most surely do . . . do that and live,"
    said Jesus . . .
        several days of planning
                jockeying for position
                calculating—
        Jesus had made him
        answer for himself—

He pressed a bit further:
    "No doubt about loving God;
    we know who *he* is . . .
        but—
            who
            is
            my
            neighbor?"

Every eye moved to Jesus for his rejoinder . . .
    he squinted in the sun's glare
        kicked a small stone with his left big toe
        and sat down on a porch step . . .
    "Let me tell you
    a story . . ."
            and insight poured forth
            like smoke
            from burning moss . . .

A man going to Jericho . . .
 attacked by thieves . . .
 beaten . . .
 robbed . . .
 left bleeding in a ditch . . .
  passing priest
   cleansed for Temple ritual
   cannot touch blood
    or death . . .
  passing Levite suspects faking robber
   rushes away
   in sweaty fear . . .
  passing Samaritan merchant stops
   binds wounds
   carries him to nearby inn
   pays for anticipated stay—
   gets credit in case of long stay!—
   assumes responsibility
    for any
    additional expenses!

Then Jesus levels *his* careful question
 to the inquisitive lawyer:
  "Now, who was neighbor
  to the man
  who fell among thieves?"
   no biting sarcasm
   no harsh ridicule
   no cynicism—
  another fair question—

The man nodded quietly.

He had it in focus—
        squarely in focus:
                not
                        "Who
                        is
                        my
                        neighbor?"
                but
                        "Whose
                        neighbor
                        am
                        I?"

A man who lived
        in the high ether
        of theory
                had encountered
                a man
                who lived
                on the low plane
                of practicality!

They parted some time later—
        the lawyer came
        with one question—
                he left
                with a sock full!

The banter with Jesus
        had been lively
        had been saturated with truth!

They gripped wrists and smiled quietly.

What I heard next
      brought a quick lump
      to my throat
         the lawyer
         looked squarely
         into Jesus' eyes
         and said:
              "Thanks, *neighbor!*"

He knew it in his deepest soul—
      he'd
         just
            met
               the
                  Good
                     Samaritan!

8 A Tribute to Thomas

My closest friend among the apostles of Jesus
    was Thomas . . .

That fact in no way means
    that he was
    easy to get to know—
        the very opposite
    was the case . . .

Our initial friction was largely due
    to the wide-eyed way
    I "forsook all and followed . . ."

I was to learn later
    that
    a great many people
    made enthusiastic responses to Jesus
        because it was popular—
            the
            "in-thing"
            to do.

Thomas was genuinely
            generally suspicious
      of anyone
      to whom
      the faith
      came easily . . .

My first efforts at friendship
      were "returned unopened . . ."
            than I was analyzed
                        debated
                        sifted
                        dissected . . .

            eventually
            I was able
            to engage him
            in conversation
                  sometimes
                  our talks lasted
                  into the morning hours . . .
            next to the long talks
            with Jesus
                  I remember
                  the ones
                  with Thomas
                  best of all . . .

Fringe-dwellers used two words
      to describe Thomas:
            cynic
                  and
            doubter . . .

We had a long talk about those words
  late one night . . .
    he became
    a significant individual
      and influence on my life
    from that night on . . .

I had just asked him:
  "How did you get
  so thirsty
  for truth?"

He smiled a slow
    deep smile
  stared at his hands
  cleared his throat
  glanced up at a bright moon
    and unraveled
    considerable knit . . .

He had been born a twin
  life is tough enough
  without someone
  looking just like you!

His brother was eager to please
    outgoing
    bright
    pleasant
  Thomas had become quiet
      pensive
      probing . . .

His brother was always praised
                    honored—
        Thomas was mildly resentful
        but he set out
        to cut a clean swath
              of his own
              in life . . .

Thomas felt it was fairly normal
        to come out of that background
        with a fair dose
        of skepticism . . .
              he had never taken
              easy answers—
                    never intended to!

One thing he said amused me:
        "We've made a Jewish folk hero
        out of Gideon
        because he put out his fleece *twice*
        before he'd follow God—
              but in reality
              you let a man
              seriously question God *once*
              and people who swallow anything
              label him a heretic!"

I had never thought about that!

Many other ideas of his
        were enormously helpful
        in my early days with Jesus . . .

For instance,
    I had always seen doubt
    as the opposite
    of belief—
        you either *doubt*
                or *believe!*
    Not so, saith Thomas . . .
        doubt was for him
        the deep companion
        of faith—
            it could bring you
            to faith
            in a more nearly
            mature way . . .
    he felt that doubt
        was a way
        to seek more factual information
        before making a commitment
        to a belief . . .

Another example was most interesting . . .
    to Thomas
    you had not really believed
    if you had merely memorized the ritual
        had merely accepted
                what heritage
                had passed down to you—
    he had absolutely no regard for tradition
    if it did not coincide with truth—
        this was the ultimate irresponsibility:
            to follow unquestioned truth
            in an unquestioning way—

Thomas referred to that
        as "the
                bland
                leading
                the
                bland!"

He also had no use for the person
        who spent his life
        just *questioning* . . .
                he could not see
                what you accomplished
                by questioning
                but never accepting any answers!
        in his opinion
                serious questioning
                could only be justified
                by affirming the answer wholeheartedly!
                        with firm conviction!
        the true test of maturity for Thomas
                was whether or not
                you were willing
                to continue to submit
                even your most profound convictions
                to continued probing . . .
                        "That's where your life
                        puts real corn
                        in the shuck . . ."
        he felt it was dangerous
                to decide too early in life
                what you'd think, believe, and do
                all the rest of it!

Thomas felt that a man
    who came to deep faith
    through intense struggle
    was probably best equipped
    to help other strugglers:
        he referred to this
        as:
            "One beggar
            showing another beggar
            where he found bread!"

That conversation that night pivoted my life!

It did not surprise me at all after that
    that Thomas reacted
    as he did
    to the news
    of Jesus' resurrection
    from the dead—
        our world had caved in Friday—
    it was the worst day of my life . . .

Thomas and I had gone to a high bluff
    overlooking the Jordan valley
    to let our souls bleed . . .
        we were found
        by Bartholomew
        who had been running about
        trying to find us—

The news was incredible!
    Jesus was alive!

Rushing toward town I could not contain
        my excitement!
        my joy!
        my hope!
                Thomas walked fast
                but without comment . . .

After two furious hours of walking
        we stopped to rest
        for a few moments . . .
                we sat down
                beneath a large fig tree . . .
                        "Do you think
                        it could *really*
                        be true,
                        Thomas?"
                He shrugged his shoulders:
                        "Don't know, Norton . . .
                        I'll have to see it
                                to believe it!"
                Then he added—
                        almost under his breath—
                    "But,
                    if I see it—
                    I'll believe it!"

And I hurried on with him—
        before
        his
        fleece
        could
        dry . . .

Backword

Thanks for taking time to come to know Norton.

In case you still wonder
about him
let me tell you a quick story . . .

Will Rogers wrote a regular column
for several years
for the *New York Times.*

His language was rustic . . .
his grammar was poor . . .
his spelling was pathetic!
    (Example:
        diddent for *didn't*
        wuzzint for *wasn't*)

The first column he wrote
came off the press
as though Will *Shakespeare* . . .
        not Will *Rogers* . . .
had written it!

Editors had respelled and regrammared
until Will didn't (or, *diddent*)
recognize it.

He called the editor.

In essence, he said that people
wo i'd know he didn't write it
bec ause it was correct!
            He insisted that it be left
            in rustic
                        ungrammatical
                        misspelled form
in order to preserve authenticity
and fun!

Without knocking the King James Version
of the Bible
my basic opinion is
that Simon and Andrew and Jesus
would not recognize themselves
in such precise language.

THE GOSPEL ACCORDING TO NORTON
is my honest effort
to recreate the feelings
                        joys
                        hurts
                        pains
                        smells
                        noises
of ordinary people
touching the life of
the most extraordinary of all men . . .
            Jesus of Nazareth.

My prayer is that *he* may be fully human
in a more real way
because you have come to know Norton . . .
    further,
    I pray that *you* will be more fully human
    because you have
    a bit more fully
    come to know
    Jesus of Nazareth!

Peace!